MY PERSONALITY

By Mary McGuiness

An introduction to the personality types
described by Carl Jung and Isabel Myers.

Published in Australia by
MaryMac Books

CONTENTS

HOW TO USE THIS BOOK

This book was written for children aged about 7-10 years to introduce them to some of the natural personality differences in people and to encourage an appreciation of differences. It has been designed to be used in an interactive and fun way with a teacher or parent guiding the learning. See page 24 for more information.

Published by:
MaryMac Books
P.O. Box 715
Cherrybrook NSW Australia 2126
www.itd.net.au
Email: marymcg@itd.net.au

Artwork: Dave Hackett

PUBLISHED IN AUSTRALIA

International Standards Book Number: 0 9751888 3 6

PEOPLE ARE DIFFERENT IN MANY, MANY WAYS

We're all Different!

Some people are tall, some are short.
Some people are good athletes. Others may not enjoy physical activity.
Some people are good at handling animals. Some people are scared of animals.
Some people read very quickly. Other may find reading difficult.
Some people have a great sense of humour. Others are more serious.
Some people dance well. Others people would rather watch.
Some people may have beliefs that are different from your family.
Some people have different customs and may wear different clothes.
Some people like to perform on stage. Some people would never do that.

Can you add some interesting difference you have noticed in people...

Differences make us interesting!

Likes to Daydream
_____

Can cook
_____

Speaks more than one Language
_____

Likes noise, parties and Music
_____

Collects cards, stamps or other things
_____

Is good at Maths or Science
$- \times \div +$
_____

Sings or plays Music
_____

Likes to Dance
_____

MY FRIENDS AND FAMILY

Write the name of a friend or family member who fits the description in each box...

Looks after animals
_____

Likes to come top of the class
_____

Keeps all his/her things tidy and Organised
_____

Is good at sport
_____

Enjoys poetry and stories
_____
Stories   Poems

Has a messy bedroom
_____

Likes to look after people
_____

Likes spending time alone
_____

GIFTS AND ABILITIES

Start by drawing or pasting a picture of a member of your family in each box. Then with each person, draw or paste a picture of something that represents their talent.

I juggle goldfish... What's your special talent?

I can tell the future with my toenail clippings!

Toe Nails

Things I am
good at...

_____
_____
_____
_____
_____

Draw or paste a picture here

My friends say I'm good at...

WHO

name _____

Good things my parents say about me...

_____
_____
_____
_____
_____

YOU ROCK!

What kind of person am I?

_____
_____
_____
_____
_____
_____
_____

?

When I grow up I would like to be or do...

_____

_____

_____

_____

_____

_____

Say Aaah!

My favourite Things...

_____

_____

_____

_____

_____

AM I?

My age _____   Gender _____

My favourite activities, sports, hobbies and things to do...

_____

_____

_____

_____

_____

Abilities I want to develop

_____

_____

_____

_____

_____

_____

MY HEROES

Famous people or characters from stories, cartoons and movies. In each frame, put a picture of someone you admire, and write what you like about them.

Name:
Talents:

Name:
Talents:

Name:
Talents:

Name:
Talents:

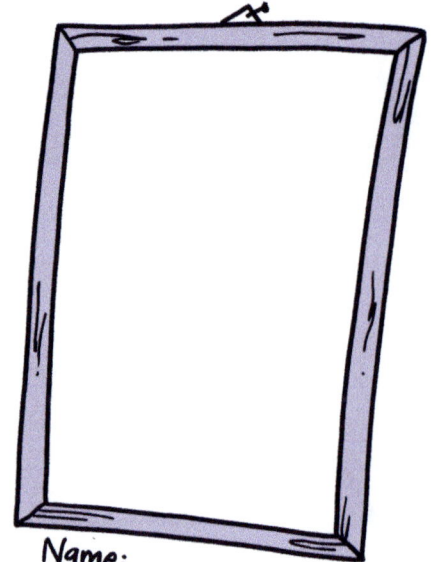

Name:
Talents:

Name:
Talents:

PERSONALITY

Every person is born with certain personality characteristics. You may have noticed that you are very much like some people you know and very different from other people. These differences are natural. Personality differences are gifts that make it easy for us to develop some special talents and abilities.

Personality affects many things in life. Some examples are:

- how we relate to people or animals
- the way we learn
- the hobbies we choose
- the books we read
- what we want to achieve in life
- what we like to do in our free time

We are going to look at some important natural differences in people. These differences will help you to understand your friends, your teachers and your family.

The four areas of personality we will explore are:

- how we get our energy
- how we learn
- how we make choices
- how we organise our things

WHERE DO I GET MY ENERGY FROM?

Choose the one from each pair that describes YOU best:

☐ Active
△ Calm

△ Prefer a quiet classroom
☐ Learn best with others

☐ Like being with groups
△ Like being alone

△ Making new friends is hard
☐ Making new friends is easy

△ Listen
☐ Talk

☐ Doing things with others
△ Thinking about things

☐ Outgoing
△ Private

☐ Like meeting new people
△ Prefer people I know

Hey, are you OUTGOING?

No, I'm just GOING OUT!

☐ Like to have lots of friends
△ Like a few special friends

△ Quiet
☐ Talkative

☐ **Extraversion**
Some people like to be around other people most of the time. They get energy from the outer world of activity, noise and people. They find it easy to get to know people. This preference is called *Extraversion*.

△ **Introversion**
Some people like to spend a lot of time alone or with someone they know well. They get energy from their inner world of thoughts, ideas and feelings. They like privacy. This preference is called *Introversion*.

Score: ☐ __   △ __

10

We can all be both OUTGOING and PRIVATE, but one is more natural.

**EXTRAVERSION
(OUTGOING)**

**INTROVERSION
(PRIVATE)**

People or characters I know who
are OUTGOING:

_____
_____
_____
_____
_____

People or characters I know
who are PRIVATE:

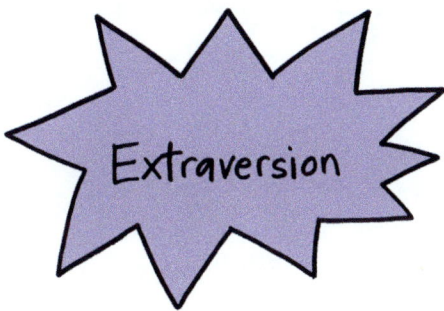

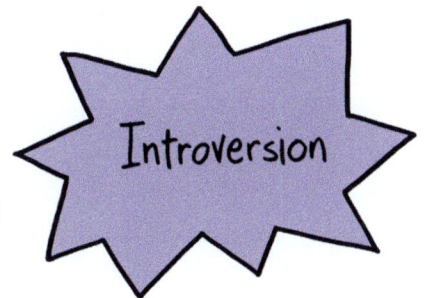

_____
_____
_____
_____
_____

Which one is
most like YOU?

Extraversion

Introversion

Undecided

HOW DO I LEARN?

Choose the one from each pair that describes YOU best:

- ☐ Want clear instructions
- △ Want to do it my way

- △ Like using my imagination
- ☐ Like using what I know

- △ Dreaming
- ☐ Doing

- △ Enjoy make believe stories
- ☐ Enjoy real stories

- ☐ Like to make or fix things
- △ Like to invent things

- ☐ Now
- △ Future

- ☐ Like to use my hands to do things
- △ Like to try new ideas

I rely on my five senses to learn!

I had a hunch you were going to say that!

- △ Possibilities
- ☐ Reality

- ☐ Like facts
- △ Like ideas

- △ Like to try new and different things
- ☐ Like to do things I have done before

Sensing
☐ Some people use their five senses to gather facts about the real world. They notice details like colour, shapes, sounds, smells and numbers. They are more interested in what is happening now than in the future. This preference is called *Sensing*.

Intuition
△ Some people use their imagination to get ideas. They like ideas that are new and different. They prefer to dream about the future. They are more interested in what is possible in the future than in facts and reality. This preference is called *Intuition*.

Score: ☐___ △___

We can all use both SENSING and INTUITION, but one is more natural.

O.K... I have the instructions, and all the parts — this feels like it's going to work!

BUILD IT YOURSELF!

PAINT PAI PXi

SENSING (REALITY)

INTUITION (IMAGINATION)

People or characters I know who are REALISTIC and PRACTICAL:

_____
_____
_____
_____
_____

People or characters I know who are IMAGINATIVE and INVENTIVE:

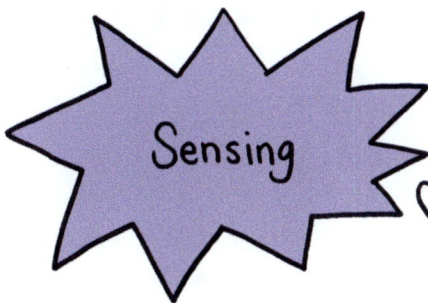

_____
_____
_____
_____
_____

Which one is most like YOU?

Sensing

Intuition

Undecided

HOW DO I MAKE DECISIONS?

Choose the one from each pair that describes YOU best:

- ☐ Do the right thing
- △ Make people happy

- △ Making friends
- ☐ Winning

- ☐ Thinking
- △ Feeling

- ☐ Rules
- △ People

- ☐ Like clever people
- △ Like caring people

- △ Helping People
- ☐ Solving Problems

- △ Try not to hurt people's feelings
- ☐ Say what I think is right

- ☐ Fair
- △ Kind

- ☐ Talk about what I know
- △ Talk about how I feel

DON'T PARK HERE— IT'S THE RULE

YOU CAN PARK HERE, AS LONG AS IT'S O.K WITH EVERYONE ELSE

- ☐ Like teachers who know a lot
- △ Like teachers who care about people

☐ **Thinking**
Some people use logic to make decisions. They think about what is right and what the rules say. They want to be successful and usually like competition. They admire people who are clever and expect people to be fair. This preference is called *Thinking*.

△ **Feeling**
Some people use their values to make decisions. They think about how their decisions will affect people, animals and nature. They care about other people and want to make them happy. They admire people who are kind and friendly. This preference is called *Feeling*.

Score: ☐___ △___

14

We can all use both THINKING and FEELING, but one is usually easier.

If I can move there... in five moves I'll win!

THINKING (LOGIC)

We're such good friends

We really appreciate each other

FEELING (VALUES)

People or characters I know who choose what is the RIGHT thing to do:

_____
_____
_____
_____
_____

People or characters I know who choose what is BEST FOR PEOPLE:

_____
_____
_____
_____
_____

Thinking

Which one is most like YOU?

Feeling

Undecided

AM I ORGANISED OR SPONTANEOUS?

Choose the one from each pair that describes YOU best:

☐ Keep my things organised
△ Put my things anywhere

△ Play first
☐ Work first

☐ Like a teacher who is organised
△ Like a teacher who is fun

△ Like surprises
☐ Like to know what's happening

☐ Follow the rules
△ Like to change the rules

☐ I enjoy finishing projects
△ I don't always finish things

☐ Always plan ahead
△ Just go

△ Have trouble deciding
☐ Decide things quickly

I'm planning my LIFE!

Me too!

CALENDAR

DIARY

☐ Like plans and timetables
△ I do things when I want

△ Often late
☐ Get things done on time

Organised (Judging)
☐ Some people are naturally organised. They can easily keep their things in order. They finish projects on time and are always punctual. They make decisions quickly. They like to plan ahead of time and don't like to change their plans. This preference is called *Judging*.

Spontaneous (Perceiving)
△ Some people are naturally spontaneous and flexible. They can easily change their plans. They like surprises and enjoy following their curiosity. They like to have choices when they do projects. They find it difficult to make decisions when both choices are interesting. This preference is called *Perceiving*.

Score: ☐___ △___

We can all be both ORGANISED and SPONTANEOUS, but one is usually easier.

TIMETABLE

THIS is the PLAN!

Sure! I don't mind how we do it!

JUDGING
(ORGANISED)

PERCEIVING
(SPONTANEOUS)

People or characters I know who are ORGANISED:

_____

_____

_____

_____

_____

People or characters I know who are SPONTANEOUS:

_____

_____

_____

_____

_____

Which one is most like YOU?

Judging

Perceiving

Undecided

MY PERSONALITY

I prefer...

E	**U**	**I**
Extraversion	**Undecided**	**Introversion**
Outgoing		Private
Action		Quiet

S	**U**	**N**
Sensing	**Undecided**	**Intuition**
Reality		Imagination
Facts		Possibilities

T	**U**	**F**
Thinking	**Undecided**	**Feeling**
Logic		Values
Fairness		People

J	**U**	**P**
Judging	**Undecided**	**Perceiving**
Organised		Spontaneous
Planned		Adaptable

My four preferences are _____ _____ _____ _____

Each preference is a gift.

WHAT HELPS ME TO LEARN?

Extraverted students (E)
Like activity, doing things
Learn by interacting with people
Use trial and error
Talk first, then reflect
Get ideas and information from the world around them

Introverted students (I)
Need regular quiet time
Enjoy working alone or in pairs
Can concentrate for long periods
Reflect quietly first, then speak
Look inside for information and ideas

Sensing students (S)
Focus on facts and details
Trust experience
Use a step-by-step method
Use language literally
Need clear instructions
Need practical, real examples first

iNtuitive students (N)
Focus on possibilities
Like to use the imagination
Mind works in skips and jumps
Enjoy interpretation and symbols
Look for patterns and inspiration
Prefer concepts first, then practical

Thinking students (T)
Interested in logic and analysis
Need freedom to think their own ideas
Need to achieve in intellectual, mechanical or technical areas
Need praise for competence
Expect teachers to be competent
Make decisions with logic

Feeling students (F)
Interested in people & relationships
Like to help and understand people
The need for approval and support is greater than the need to achieve
Need praise for effort and helpfulness
Need harmony with teachers & class
Make decisions with their values

Judging students (J)
Need structure and predictability
Enjoy finishing things
Want a clear work plan
Want accountability
Can handle variety within a structure

Perceiving students (P)
Need variety and flexibility
Want to remain open to new data
Need to follow their curiosity
Need autonomy and real choices
Will accept structure if they have choices within it

SJ   Guardian-Stabilizer

Needs: Belonging
            Structure and order
            Responsibility

ISFJ

ISFJ children are quiet, realistic, caring and organised. They prefer doing practical things more than using the imagination. They are responsible and cooperative. They usually like timetables, rules, routine and uniforms.

Favourite activities often include:
• practical - likes cooking, knitting or craft
• physical activities like sport and dancing
• playing a musical instrument
• helping parents or doing things for people
• belonging to groups like Scouts, Guides
• reading real life stories

Learning: ISFJs learn through experience and by practising skills. They need harmony and order in the classroom. They need learning related to real life and clear instructions. They may talk in class but prefer to study alone. They like to read real life stories about people more than fantasy.

ESFJ

ESFJ children are outgoing, realistic, caring and organised. They are responsible and cooperative. They enjoy caring for people or animals. They need harmony and approval and avoid conflict. They like timetables, rules and uniforms.

Favourite activities often include:
• practical - like cooking, art or craft
• physical activities like sport and athletics
• singing, dancing or drama
• helping parents or doing things for people
• organising other children to perform
• playing a musical instrument

Learning: ESFJs learn through experience and interaction. They need harmony and order in the classroom. They need learning related to real life and clear instructions. They have a good memory for facts, especially about people. They like to read real life stories about people more than fantasy.

ISTJ

ISTJ children are quiet, observant, logical and organised. They prefer practical things more than using the imagination. They are responsible and cooperative. They usually like timetables, rules, routine and uniforms.

Favourite activities often include:
• practical - like cooking or making things
• physical activities like sport and dancing
• reading or playing a musical instrument
• helping parents or fixing things
• belonging to groups like Scouts, Guides
• collecting stamps, rocks or football cards

Learning: ISTJs learn through experience and by practising skills. They need order and quiet in the classroom. They need learning related to real life and clear instructions. They need to see a practical use for what they are learning. They have a good memory for facts and details. They like to read about facts and real life more than fantasy.

ESTJ

ESTJ children are outspoken, practical, logical and organised. They are very curious and want logical reasons for what they are doing. They like to organise their belongings and keep things in their right place. They need achievement and activity.

Favourite activities often include:
• making or fixing things
• collecting things like cars or baseball caps
• physical activities like team sport and athletics
• playing music
• helping parents with practical things at home
• computers, games

Learning: ESTJs learn through experience and by asking questions. They need to see a practical use for what they are learning. They need clear instructions. They have a good memory for things they find interesting. They need order, routine and feedback. They are interested in books about facts and real life more than fantasy.

SP   Artisan-Negotiator

Needs: Freedom
            Action
            Fun

ESFP
ESFP children are playful, active, realistic, fun-loving and spontaneous. They care about people and have strong values. They are energetic performers. They need freedom, action and fun. They need boundaries but don't like a lot of rules.
Favourite activities often include:
- acting, singing or playing music
- sport, team games, and outdoor activities
- collecting toys, rocks or football cards
- comedy, practical jokes, magic tricks
- building mechanical things or Lego
- computer games or transformers, gadgets

Learning: ESFPs learn more by doing than by listening or reading. They use language literally so they need specific instructions and real life examples. Learning needs to use the senses and have a purpose. They may have difficulty imagining. They prefer books with action, realistic stories about people, or how things work.

ISFP
ISFP children are quiet, realistic, caring and spontaneous. They care about people and animals and have strong values. They need freedom, action and fun and don't like a lot of rules. They enjoy time alone and dislike conflict.
Favourite activities often include:
- individual sports, outdoor activities,
- acting, singing or playing music
- collecting toys, rocks or football cards
- comedy, practical jokes, magic tricks
- building mechanical things or Lego
- gadgets, drawing and craft

Learning: ISFPs learn more by doing than by listening or reading. They use language literally so they need specific instructions and real life examples. Learning needs to use the senses and have a purpose. To concentrate they need quiet. Imagining may be difficult. They prefer books with action, how things work, or real stories about people.

ESTP
ESTP children are energetic, realistic, logical spontaneous and interested in everything. They are logical and assertive. They enjoy the limelight and need freedom, action and fun. They need boundaries but don't like rules and structure.
Favourite activities often include:
- sport, team games, outdoor activities
- collecting toys, rocks or football cards
- building mechanical things, Lego, Rubics cubes
- computer games or transformer toys
- comedy, practical jokes, magic tricks
- acting, singing or playing music

Learning: ESTPs learn more by doing than by listening or reading. They use language literally so they need specific instructions and real life examples. Learning needs to use the senses and have a purpose. They may have difficulty imagining. They read books on how things work, books with action, or realistic adventure stories.

ISTP
ISTP children are quiet, realistic, logical and spontaneous. They like a variety of practical things to do. They need freedom, action and fun and don't like a lot of rules. They enjoy time alone observing and analysing things in their minds.
Favourite activities often include:
- watching or playing individual sports
- outdoor activities
- using tools, craft, gadgets
- comedy, practical jokes, magic tricks
- building mechanical things or fixing things
- computer games, solving mathematical problems

Learning: ISTPs learn by doing more than by listening or reading. They use language literally so they need specific instructions and real life examples. Learning needs to use the senses and have a purpose. Imagining may be difficult. They need quiet for concentration. They read books on how things work, or real life adventure stories.

NF   Idealist-Catalyst

Needs: Relationships
             Harmony, meaning
             Self-understanding

ENFP
ENFP children are enthusiastic, imaginative, caring and spontaneous. They are outgoing and enjoy activities that are new and creative. They often enjoy singing and performing. They usually make friends easily and dislike conflict.

Favourite activities often include:
• playing music, singing and dancing
• acting, role-playing or dressing up
• reading and daydreaming
• art
• creative writing
• some team games and team sports

Learning: ENFPs enjoy learning that stimulates the imagination and allows them to be creative. They often need to discuss ideas to understand, so they enjoy group work. They learn easily from books. They can express their ideas clearly in writing or verbally. They need harmony. They enjoy reading about people or magical places.

ENFJ
ENFJ children are enthusiastic, imaginative, caring and organised. They are outgoing and talkative. They like to organise and care for other people. They are cooperative and eager to please. They need harmony and avoid conflict.

Favourite activities often include:
• singing, dancing and playing music
• acting, role-playing and dressing up
• using the imagination, make-believe play
• art and craft
• reading, creative writing, listening to stories
• organising other children to play and perform

Learning: ENFJs enjoy learning that stimulates the imagination and allows them to be creative. They need an interactive and supportive classroom. They like to organise and finish things. They enjoy creative writing. They see patterns and enjoy the meaning behind words. They enjoy reading about people, fantasy or poetry.

INFP
INFP children are reflective, imaginative, caring and spontaneous. They care about other people and their rights. They try to create harmony and avoid conflict. They enjoy creative activities. They need approval and like to please others.

Favourite activities often include:
• reading and daydreaming
• creative writing, diaries and poetry
• playing music, singing
• acting
• art
• being with nature

Learning: INFPs enjoy learning that uses the imagination and allows them to be creative. They usually enjoy reading and writing. They are more interested in ideas and meaning than facts. They may enjoy group work to share ideas but often prefer to work alone. They need harmony. They enjoy reading about people or magical places.

INFJ
INFJ children are quiet, imaginative, caring and organised. They enjoy using the imagination which takes them to magical kingdoms, far away places and other worlds. They usually relate well to other people but need a lot of time alone.

Favourite activities often include:
• reading books that stimulate the imagination
• reading and writing poetry
• dreaming about the future
• acting
• art, drawing images from their imagination
• being with nature and people

Learning: INFJs are independent learners. They enjoy learning that uses the imagination and look for patterns .They have very good language skills and do well in subjects where they can express their ideas in writing. They prefer to work alone. They enjoy reading that stimulates the imagination, such as poetry and mythology.

NT — Rational-Inventor

Need: Competence
Problems to solve
Freedom to think

INTP

INTP children are quiet, imaginative, logical and spontaneous. They are independent thinkers and enjoy solving problems. They are often happy alone observing and analysing things in their minds. They want to understand everything and be competent.

Favourite activities often include:
• reading to gain knowledge and understanding
• using computers and surfing the internet
• playing computer games
• logical games like chess, solving problems
• music, drama and fine arts
• martial arts

Learning: INTPs enjoy learning. They thrive if they are encouraged to think for themselves. They are abstract thinkers and need to explore ideas and solve problems. They question everything, asking 'Why?' or 'Why not?'. They read continuously on almost any ideas to gain knowledge, understanding and competence.

ENTP

ENTP children are energetic, imaginative, logical and spontaneous. They are independent thinkers and enjoy solving problems. They enjoy activities that are new, creative and use the imagination. They need to be competent at whatever they do.

Favourite activities often include:
• debating and discussing ideas
• logical games like chess, solving problems
• using computers
• reading to gain information
• music and art
• some team sports

Learning: ENTPs are independent thinkers who can express their ideas clearly and logically. They have enquiring minds. They analyse and question everything in order to understand. They need to be challenged and have problems to solve. And, they need to experience competence. They read a variety of topics in books and on the internet.

INTJ

INTJ children are quiet, imaginative, logical and organised. They enjoy using the imagination which takes them to far away places and other worlds. They organise things logically and are concerned about justice. They need a lot of time alone.

Favourite activities often include:
• reading books that stimulate the imagination
• reading and writing poetry
• dreaming about the future
• music and drama
• discussing and debating issues
• solving problems

Learning: INTJs are independent learners. They learn best in a challenging environment with periods of quiet. They value learning and need freedom to think their own thoughts. They have good language skills, especially writing. They enjoy reading that stimulates the imagination, such as poetry and mythology.

ENTJ

ENTJ children are talkative, imaginative, logical and organised. They ask lots of questions and can logically argue their point of view. They are usually outspoken, confident and very interested in problem- solving. They enjoy organising.

Favourite activities often include:
• being a leader
• reading books that stimulate the imagination
• dreaming about the future
• discussing and debating issues
• solving problems
• organising anything

Learning: ENTJs are independent learners. They learn best in a challenging environment. They value learning and need freedom to think their own thoughts. They like to solve complex problems. They have good language skills, verbal and written. They are keen readers and enjoy books that stimulates the imagination with new ideas.

FOR PARENTS AND TEACHERS

The personality theory presented in this book is based on the work of Carl Jung and Isabel Myers. The characteristics or preferences described on pages 10 to 17 indicate some natural differences in children. Each child has certain innate preferences which usually develop in either childhood or adolescence. The other preferences will usually develop during adult life. For each child some preferences will be well developed and some will be poorly developed and of little interest. Regular opportunities to use their natural preferences can ensure that learning experiences are effective and can also promote the development of the child. By contrast, learning experiences that require the constant use of poorly developed preferences result in poor learning, stress and missed opportunities to promote development.

Personality theory shows us very clearly how our interests, needs, motivations and natural learning styles differ. It also helps us to see why some students struggle to survive in the classroom and what can be done to allow students to achieve their potential and enjoy learning. The successful teacher is one who can create learning experiences that enables a child to achieve and be motivated to want to learn. The challenge for both teachers and parents is to help children to develop their natural abilities and to build their self-confidence.

Western education is preoccupied with measuring achievement, assuming that all children should be able to perform a set task by a certain age. Type theory shows why this is unrealistic. A more realistic approach is to provide a variety of learning activities, drawing on all eight preferences. In this way teachers can cater for the different learning styles, allowing every child to learn in his or her own way, and to experience success and satisfaction.

How to use this book

This book was written for children aged 7-10 years to introduce them to some of the natural personality differences in people and to encourage an appreciation of differences. It has been designed to be used in an interactive and fun way with a teacher or parent guiding the learning. The ideas covered in this book will come alive if the teacher or parent encourages discussion and uses lots of examples to illustrate the ideas presented. Examples of differences can be found in heroes in the media, celebrities in sport or children's movies and cartoon characters, as well as differences in the members of your group or family.

Children should be encouraged to discuss the ideas in this book with parents, teachers, classmates and friends. Emphasis should be on the value of differences and the gifts associated with the personality differences. Each two pages could be explored in a separate session so that the children would not be overwhelmed with too many ideas at once. The amount of time needed will vary depending on the amount of activity organised. A guide would be six or seven sessions of 40-60 minutes.

For ideas on how to present this material to young children please contact the author. Contact details are given on page 2.

Useful References

Lawrence, Gordon, (1993) People Types and Tiger Stripes, Third Edition. Gainsville FL: CAPT

McGuiness, Mary, (2004) You've Got Personality. Sydney: MaryMac Books

Murphy, Elizabeth, (1992) The Developing Child: Using Jungian Type to Understand Children. Palo Alto, CA: CPP

Myers, Isabel, (1980) Gifts Differing. Palo Alto, CA: CPP

Tieger, Paul & Barron-Tieger, Barbara, (1997) Nurture by Nature. New York City, NY: Little Brown & Co.

www.ingramcontent.com/pod-product-compliance
Lightning Source LLC
Chambersburg PA
CBHW060958030426

42334CB00032B/3281